CRUSHED

In

I0159703

SPIRIT

Help for Christians suffering from a wounded and broken spirit

And we all, with unveiled face, are being changed into his likeness from one degree of glory to another; for this comes from the Lord who is the Spirit.

2 Corinthians 3:18

Charles Pretlow

Crushed in Spirit
Help for Christians suffering from a wounded and broken spirit

Third printing July 2016
Copyright © Charles Pretlow

All scripture references and quotes are from the Revised Standard Version of the Holy Bible unless otherwise noted.
Old Testament Section Copyright © 1952
New Testament Section Copyright © 1946, 1971
by Thomas Nelson Inc.

ISBN 978-0-9801768-9-6

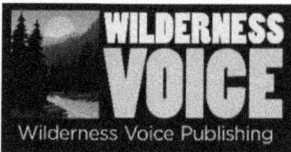

Published by -

Wilderness Voice Publishing, LLC
Canon City, Colorado USA
www.wvpbooks.com

"A voice crying in the wilderness - proclaiming the good news of the coming Kingdom!"

About
MCI Recovery Ministries

June 1988 Pastor Charles Pretlow began to counsel struggling Christians. He was appointed counseling pastor in a 400-member Foursquare fellowship and within six months of ministry, his calendar was booked three months in advance.

These troubled Christians were seeking help for a variety of issues and many learned about this new Holy Spirit led counseling by word of mouth. Most who came suffered from being reared in a dysfunctional family system; however, some cases were from severe abuse, parental abandonment, and childhood systematic sexual abuse, (termed as victims of Cult Family Ritualistic Abuse (CFRA). Over the years Pastor Pretlow also worked with victims of Satanic Ritualistic Abuse (SRA Victims).

Early on in ministry, the number of wounded Christians coming for help nearly overwhelmed Pastor Pretlow. He realized that proper understanding of Scripture and being led by the Holy Spirit in facilitating God's healing power and grace was the only way to succeed. In his study of Scripture and dependence on the Holy Spirit, he soon discovered that employing the true gifts of the Holy Spirit in counseling and teaching those in his care how to work with the Holy Spirit as counselor was the best way to help so many hurting Christians coming for help.

Unfortunately, Pastor Pretlow found that popular quick-fix teachings embraced within the Foursquare fellowship where he was ministering actually slowed recovery progress, undermining healing, growth, and maturity in Christ. He soon found it counterproductive to fight against these ingrained false teachings, and thus was led to start his own fellowship.

Pastor Pretlow found that by embracing all that Christ taught and building disciples through mentoring and counseling proved to be effective in helping struggling Christian become stable servants of Christ.

Through these many years of ministry, study, and his own recovery, specific principles in Scripture became obvious keys in helping wounded Christians become whole in Christ, and to have them learn to work with the Holy Spirit as their ultimate counselor.

Now it is time to present these principles and teachings found in Scripture, to help those called to minister to God's wounded learn to boldly declare the full counsel of God and to walk in the true gifts of the Holy Spirit.

Led by the Holy Spirit, MCI Recovery Ministries has become the platform to help facilitate others in learning how to work with the Holy Spirit in recovery. And to help train other pastors and ministries learn to be used by the Holy Spirit in implementing God's program for God's wounded who are in their care.

MCI Recovery Ministries
PO Box 857
Canon City, CO 81215

www.mcirecovery.com

Contents

Wounds and Defilements from the Past

The winds of false doctrine have indoctrinated most Christians to believe that when they become born again and come to Christ, all their issues from the past are just history—to be ignored and forgotten.

Millions of believers in Christ are taught that all past sins, defilements, and abuse are under the blood of Christ, never again to be a concern.

This includes their old manner of life, any lingering emotional and spiritual problems, demonic oppression, or temptations. Any lingering issues will vanish through simple prayer, praise or worship, faithful fellowship attendance, or more study and the memorization of Scripture, or falling under the instant deliverance power of the Holy Spirit through an anointed ministry.

To the contrary, the New Testament Scriptures clearly explain that wounds and issues from the past can be a problem to all believers, if these issues are not properly dealt with.

The New Testament principle of sanctification teaches that all true Christians must become cleansed, healed, and changed into a Christ-like person. Sanctification is a process of working out one's salvation and requires understanding and active participation with the Holy Spirit. This work requires the sincere Christian to cooperate with God's discipline, correction, and revelation of one's inner motives that do not align with God's will and standards for living.

Sanctification is a process where born-again Christians learn to obey Christ by learning of Him and his teachings and becoming transformed into His likeness by the grace of God.

It is Christ, revealing himself to the sincere Christian who wants to changed, as the 7 Apostle Paul wrote, *"Now the*

Lord is the Spirit, and where the Spirit of the Lord is, there is freedom. And we all, with unveiled face, beholding the glory of the Lord, are being changed into his likeness from one degree of glory to another; for this comes from the Lord who is the Spirit" (2 Corinthians 3:17, 18).

Unfortunately, many Christians have fallen into the same manmade rules and teachings that the Pharisees had fallen into, where Jesus declared: *"Woe to you, scribes and Pharisees, hypocrites! for you cleanse the outside of the cup and of the plate, but inside they are full of extortion and rapacity. You blind Pharisee! First cleanse the inside of the cup and of the plate, that the outside also may be clean"* (Matthew 23:25).

These false teachings today do exactly what the Pharisees were doing. They make followers of Christ believe they are magically made clean, when in reality most suffer from a heart and spirit harboring wounds and defilements. These Christians learn to put a veil over their face (become blind) and pretend they are cleaned up from their past defilements and wounds.

The Apostle Paul taught, *"Since we have these promises, beloved, let us cleanse ourselves from every defilement of body and spirit, and make holiness perfect in the fear of God"* (2 Corinthians 7:1).

Further, James wrote concerning past issues by stating, *"Cleanse your hands, you sinners, and purify your hearts, you men of double mind. Be wretched and mourn and weep. Let your laughter be turned to mourning and your joy to dejection. Humble yourselves before the Lord and he will exalt you"* (James 4:8-10).

The Cycle of Nature Set on Fire

Looking deeper into the book of James, we see the author addressing Christians who struggle in their walk with Christ. In his discourse he addresses the problem of having the whole body stained by past abuse—causing wounds to one's inner nature, citing that wrongful words will set *"on fire the cycle of nature [or wheel of birth] and set on fire by hell."* (See James 3:5, 6).

For example, let's imagine a father or mother telling their two-year-old son that because he is such a problem, they wished they never had him. Or a young teen is told that he or she is stupid and will never amount to anything because they struggle in math and received a bad grade.

These are mild examples of abuse through the tongue, but James teaches that this kind of talk actually starts a cycle of character structures to form within a child or teen, or for that matter, potentially anyone who receives such treatment.

What's more troubling, James explains that this type abuse is inflamed by the demonic (hell).

The following are a few more passages from the book of Proverbs to help clarify the seriousness of abuse and its effects on the personal spirit:

"A gentle tongue is a tree of life, but perverseness in it <u>*breaks the spirit*</u>*"* (Proverbs 15:4 underline added). The Hebrew word for *breaks* means crushed or shattered.

"A glad heart makes a cheerful countenance, but by sorrow of heart the spirit is broken" (Proverbs 15:13). In the contents of this passage, sorrow of heart does not mean a simple disappointment in life, but rather severe hopelessness and oppression in life over a prolonged period.

"Pleasant words are like a honeycomb, sweetness to the soul and health to the body" (Proverbs 16:24). In this proverb explains the effects of pleasant words in contrast to an evil-hurtful tongue. Many suffer in childhood from seasons of abuse from harmful words, while at other stages of growth they receive pleasant

words that helped developed a healthier inner nature and attitudes of heart. Unfortunately, the use of a gentle tongue will not totally heal or reverse the harm from evil words.

"A cheerful heart is a good medicine, but a downcast spirit dries up the bones" (Proverbs 17:22). Sorrow of heart and a crushed and downcast spirit can cause serious physical illness. We now understand that the marrow or center of our bones is an integral part of our immune system and is a vital in helping our body produce healthy blood cells.

Solomon was given great insight from the Lord into how influential our emotions and spirit are upon the immune system.

"A man's spirit will endure sickness; but a broken spirit who can bear?" (Proverbs 18:14). Many are entering the mental health system in an attempt to find relief through psychotherapy, counseling, and prescribed anti-psychotic drugs and anti-depressants. All this in the hope to cope with the mounting stress in their lives.

Because they suffer from a broken spirit many are now losing their emotional and mental balance. More and more people are demonstrating symptoms of mental and emotional illness and instability.

"Fathers, do not provoke your children, lest they become discouraged" (Colossians 3:21). *"Fathers, do not provoke your children to anger, but bring them up in the discipline and instruction of the Lord"* (Ephesians 6:4). Many parents provoke their children to anger through neglect, abandonment, and abuse.

Through the years of growing up, these moments of frustration produce anger that settles within the heart, mind, and spirit creating bitterness, selfishness, and sinful attitudes which gives opportunity to Satan, to influence character development and inspire sinfulness. *"Be angry but do not sin; do not let the sun go down on your anger, and give no opportunity to the devil"* (Ephesians 4:26, 27).

For a person reared in this type of environment—provoked to anger frequently without proper resolution, understanding, and forgiveness—Satan is given opportunity to misguide, tempt, and create strongholds of defilements, cancerous emotional wounds. These strongholds often carry misbeliefs about God, self, and others. (In general, through neglect and abuse the devil finds place to develop a distorted outlook on life within one's heart, mind, and spirit).

Through many years of pastoral counseling I have helped wounded Christians deal with extreme abuse from the past, not just verbal, but physical, emotional, and sexual. In some cases, torture from what I term 'cult family systems' and even satanic ritualistic abuses were revealed.

Most that I counseled were sincere Christians who sought out help after trying all the canned quick-fix formulas such as mentioned previously—praise, worship, meditation, deliverance and casting out the symptoms and so forth.

In their attempts to find inner peace and the joy of the Lord, inevitably–sooner than later the demonic attacks, overwhelming emotions, along with overwhelming temptations gained the upper hand.

Few are instructed in sound doctrine to help become whole as outlined in the book of James and other passages concerning a crushed spirit and a double-minded condition.

Thus, these sincere Christians are stumbling in the dark trying to overcome doubts and unbelief while seeking help and getting the run-around. They wonder why they suffer extra and why very few prayers are answered.

As James declares, *"But let him ask in faith, with no doubting, for he who doubts is like a wave of the sea that is driven and tossed by the wind. For that person must not suppose that a double-minded man, unstable in all his ways, will receive anything from the Lord"* (James 1:6-8 underline added).

The term *double-minded* has been misunderstood by most theologians and pastors. Here James describes the true condition—double-minded does not simply mean vacillating between two opinions or indecisive as so many believe.

Double-Minded Condition
Divided soul -or- split personality

The word double-minded is from the Greek word *dipsuchos*, and in Vine's Expository Dictionary of Biblical Words this Greek word *"dipsuchos"* as literally meaning "two-souled" (dis, "twice," *psuchē*, "a soul") or divided in soul. Young's Literal Translation of the Bible properly translates *dipsuchos* as two-souled (twice-a-soul is the direct translation in Vine's). In modern terms, James is referring to double-minded Christians as having a dual persona or a split personality.

Our soul contains our conscious mind, the spirit of our mind (unconscious and subconscious mind) and the heart, and our heart is the seat of our emotions. Another aspect of doubled-mindedness taken from the Old Testament is that the personal spirit can be wounded, broken and even crushed, in some cases crushed in pieces.

Thus, being doubled-minded means one suffers from divisions within and between the mind, heart and spirit.

Contrary to false doctrine, when one is born again, a divided state can exist in the old carnal nature, soul and personal spirit. In addition, this divided condition is not magically swept away instantly at the born-again experience.

A divided heart or split in the core inner being is the most severe issue for the divided Christian. Like King Saul in the Old Testament, the Christian with a divided or double heart can become very obsessive and even suffer from a jealous, murderous attitude of heart (Psalm 12:2). Overcoming this condition is paramount to a healthy and fulfilled life in Christ.

Peter was double-minded and in denial of his condition. In Peter's case we find that when Jesus warned Peter about Satan's desire to sift him, Jesus addressed Peter in a very enlightening way.

Jesus said, *"Simon, Simon, behold, Satan demanded to have you, that he might sift you like wheat, but I have prayed for you that your faith may not fail; and when you have turned again, strengthen your brethren"* (Luke 22:31,32 note the underlined word *you*).

The Greek word Christ used in this passage for the word *you*, in saying *Satan demanded to have you,* and further on in this verse, to *sift you like wheat* is in these two occurrences <u>plural</u>, not singular, meaning the *two of you* — or, *both of you.*

But where Christ says, *but I have prayed for you,* this use for the word *you* in the Greek is <u>singular</u>, that is, *one of you.*

This helps us understand how the double-minded condition can have true dividedness of personality and character.

Part of the challenge, as we see in Peter's case is that most that are in a *two souled* or *twice-a-soul* condition have a natural denial mechanism.

If you read the rest of the account when Peter informs Christ that he was, *"ready to go with you to prison and death,"* Jesus tells Peter what will really happen.

Denial concerning dividedness is a major obstacle to overcome—especially today where dividedness has become a mental illness label, rather than identified as a symptom of a wounded and crushed spirit and a twice-a-soul condition caused from past emotional and spiritual trauma and defilements.

Sorrow and Hardness of Heart

"Hope deferred makes the heart sick, but a desire fulfilled is a tree of life" (Proverbs 13:12).

Broken promises, parental abandonment, absentee fathers and mothers (TV often becomes the babysitter and a surrogate parent), rejection, false guilt, hypocrisy, shame, (especially if abuse is included) are major issues that destroy hope and enthusiasm for life; to grow emotionally, to learn, and to mature in character.

This kind dysfunctional and/or abusive family life makes the heart become hopeless and full of bitter sorrow and eventually hardens the heart. One raised in this environment develops resentfulness, bitter expectations, and self-loathing as well as many other emotional, mental and twisted character issues. Self-indulgence, narcissism and mild to extreme splitting are some of the consequences.

Due to the shame associated with these dysfunctional attributes, most learn to cover up the symptoms and learn to put on a "happy face." This helps survivors of abuse feel somewhat good about themselves and get along with schoolmates, neighborhood families, and society in general.

Hardness of heart is a protective barrier and often takes the form as an outer personality that others come in contact with.

Depending on the demands to be good, to be perfect, and to perform well in order to be liked and accepted—multiple personalities are often created and then are queued up or switched into action. Personality switching takes place as circumstances dictate. (Most switching between personalities is automatic or unconsciously performed.)

This is an automatic protection system and is part a hardened heart and how a wounded and divided soul and spirit is maintained in a state of balance (equilibrium).

Willfulness, rebellion, acting out, disassociation and dissociative disorders along with various dysfunctions and learning disabilities become subtle tell-tale indicators, and in many cases lead to extreme disorders of the mind and emotions.

Down Cast Spirit and Depression

"A cheerful heart is a good medicine, but a downcast spirit dries up the bones" (Proverbs 17:22). The word of God gives insight on the effects of a downcast spirit. Millions spend billions on medication and psychotherapy to counteract depression, while few understand that the most frequent reason for depression is a downcast spirit.

Other medical maladies can also be directly related to depression that Scripture identifies as the result of a downcast spirit.

Many Christians suffer from chronic depression not understanding that a major symptom of a crushed spirit that can become perpetually downcast.

Properly dealing with wounds to the spirit from past forgotten or suppressed abuse brings restoration. *"The LORD is near to the brokenhearted, and saves the crushed in spirit"* (Psalm 34:18).

Part of being saved by Christ is also becoming sanctified and made whole: *"May the God of peace himself sanctify you wholly; and may your spirit and soul and body be kept sound and blameless at the coming of our Lord Jesus Christ. He who calls you is faithful, and he will do it"* (1 Thessalonians 5:23, 24).

Few are taught how to cooperate with the Lord in the sanctifying work of the Holy Spirit that includes cleansing and healing of a wounded and a defiled spirit and a broken heart—to include revealing the hidden motives and intentions of the heart.

Sin and Defilements of Body and Spirit

Many who are crushed in spirit fall into gross sin and defile themselves in various perverse lifestyles before they are awakened by the Holy Spirit to receive salvation in Christ.

A sinful lifestyle compounds a crushed spirit with more defilements, often creating layer upon layer of inner character structures that act as avenues to demonic influences. In many cases demonic infestation grows to a point where demons are able to cohabitate with the unsuspecting person—even as a Christian.

Since many Christians do not understand how to crucify the works of the flesh and recover from a twice-a-soul condition, demonic oppression and cohabitation has become a common condition among many believers, even Christians in leadership and those supposedly baptized in the Holy Spirit.

In the case of cohabitation, the demonic spirits live within the doorways of the crushed and defiled human spirit, leaching off the person's life, finding rest and opportunity to promote and inspire trouble within the divided or double minded Christian's life.

Many wounded and crushed Christians have deep roots of bitterness; with jealousy and selfish ambition functioning as inner prime motives for living. This condition causes most to succumb to their old carnal nature that is still infected by past defilements.

James addressed this condition when he wrote the following: *"But if you have <u>bitter jealousy and selfish ambition in your hearts</u>, do not boast and be false to the truth. This wisdom is not such as comes down from above, but is <u>earthly, unspiritual, devilish</u>. For where jealousy and selfish ambition exist, there will be <u>disorder and every vile practice</u>. But the wisdom from above is first pure, then peaceable, gentle, open to reason, full of mercy and good fruits, without uncertainty or insincerity. And the harvest of righteousness is sown in peace by those who make peace."* (James 4:14-18 underline added).

Worldly and unspiritual Christians who suffer from a crushed spirit are strewn throughout the body of Christ and actually thrive in just about every fellowship. These double-minded Christians are driven and empowered by the demonic cohabitating incognito (in disguise), living in the divided fissures of the defiled and crushed human spirit and soul.

Many in this state complain some; however, these Christians seldom experience the demonic thrashing or driving them to sever instability because the demonic is in a state of cohabitation. In this state, hidden issues of heart and twisted character issues work with the demonic, and the demonic rarely choose to give up a human home unless they have to.

Many Christians in this condition learn to live as subtle trouble makers leaving a trail of disorder and chaos.

As Jude wrote, *"These are blemishes on your love feasts, as they boldly carouse together, looking after themselves; waterless clouds, carried along by winds; fruitless trees in late autumn, twice dead,* uprooted; [13]*wild waves of the sea, casting up the foam of their own shame; wandering stars for whom the nether gloom of darkness has been reserved for ever... These are grumblers, malcontents, following their own passions, loud-mouthed boasters, flattering people to gain advantage. But you must remember, beloved, the predictions of the apostles of our Lord Jesus Christ; they said to you, 'In the last time there will be scoffers, following their own ungodly passions.' It is these who set up divisions, worldly people, devoid of the Spirit"* (Jude 12-19).

This situation is widespread and few in leadership understand the serious damage, disruption, or disorder that is often incited by these troubled Christians.

Leadership and the sincere but wounded Christian must learn to follow the Apostle Paul's admonition:

"Since we have these promises, beloved, let us cleanse ourselves from every defilement of body and spirit, and make holiness perfect in the fear of God" (2 Corinthians 7:1).

Further, James makes it clear on how to overcome these issues when he states, *"Submit yourselves therefore to God. Resist the devil and he will flee from you. Draw near to God and he will draw near to you. Cleanse your hands, you sinners, and purify your hearts, you men of double mind. Be wretched and mourn and weep. Let your laughter be turned to mourning and your joy to dejection. Humble yourselves before the Lord and he will exalt you"* (James 4:7-10).

Here we read in James that the devil is close to the double-minded (twice-a-soul) Christian and sinning is prominent due to lack of cleansing, purity of heart, and a divided condition.

Breaking Denial and Hardness

To survive through life's demands while struggling with a crushed spirit requires a process of disassociation, denial, and repression of memories and feelings. This process over time is another aspect of a hardened heart and spirit.

Protective layers of feelings, thoughts and beliefs become an alternate reality in life, ensuring the painful truth stays walled off from conscious awareness. Unfortunately, this alternate set of feelings, beliefs, and subsequent thinking come from crippled character structures and carry side effects.

Life is often unstable, with emotional mood swings, unhealthy desires, and all manner of problems. Try as one might in pursuing a healthy, successful, and productive life— the symptoms from a crushed and wounded spirit become a drag.

Instead of seeking help and understanding, a hardening of the ways become automatic, where true emotions and motives are kept hidden to protect the inner person, or personal spirit from any further damage.

The need to protect self and maintain a sense of well-being and shore up an insecure ego becomes a very strong self-defense mechanism. In addition, an *absolute unconscious self-awareness blockage* sets in or, in other terms becomes a natural avoidance of truth, and this self-defense mechanism is called *denial*.

This protection mechanism of denial and calloused emotions (hardened heart) must be interrupted with truth if there is hope for healing, change, and wholeness. Often a nervous or emotional breakdown starts to occur as one of the first signs observed in breaking denial and opening up the hardened layers of character and numbed emotions.

Unfortunately, few understand what is happening to them when the pressures of life begin to break down denial.

Many Christians suffering from wounds to their personal spirit complain of feeling very distant from God and find it difficult to understand why. The Apostle Paul identifies this reason as he explains to the Christians at Ephesus:

"Now this I affirm and testify in the Lord, that you must no longer live as the Gentiles do, in the futility of their minds; they are <u>darkened in their understanding</u>, <u>alienated from the life of God</u> because of the <u>ignorance that is in them</u>, <u>due to their hardness of heart</u>; they have <u>become callous</u> and have given themselves up to licentiousness, greedy to practice every kind of uncleanness. You did not so learn Christ! — assuming that you have heard about him and were taught in him, as the truth is in Jesus. Put off your old nature which belongs to your former manner of life and is corrupt through deceitful lusts, and <u>be renewed in the spirit of your minds</u>, and put on the new nature, created after the likeness of God in true righteousness and holiness" (Ephesians 4:17-24 underlined added).

Here the Apostle Paul lays the basic reasons why so many Christian struggle with their relationship with God. Their understanding of God is limited due to the hardness of their hearts.

Further, Paul explains that they must deal with issues in their unconscious mind—that is, issues that are hidden in the spirit of their minds. Many attempt to understand their unconscious mind by going to a psychologist and or attempt to change their irrational behavior by seeking therapy from a psychiatrist.

Secular Psychology Cannot Cleanse and Heal

Millions of Christians run to secular psychology for help and only a few truly receive the kind of freedom that the Apostle Paul described in the previous passage quoted from Ephesians. Most sense something is amiss within their unconscious being, but lack understanding of scriptural principles concerning inner cleansing and healing.

Only Christ and the counsel of the Holy Spirit can shine the light of truth into the inner depths of the spirit of the mind, the inner personal spirit and the hardened heart (in many cases a divided mind and heart).

Once one receives insight and understanding concerning the root causes of the troubling symptoms, Christ is able to bring truth, facilitate true cleansing (catharsis) that resolves (not suppresses or ignores) the inner conflicts, and heals, comforts, and restores to wholeness.

The Lord is the one who created us, and He certainly knows how to heal us emotionally, mentally, and spiritually. It is our responsibility to seek Him, study the word of God and allow Him to work in our lives to change and heal us—in His way and in His timing.

Self-Pity—Satan's Stronghold

Unfortunately, many are simply pitied by most psychiatric help and pastoral counseling. Symptoms are minimized and managed through prescribed drugs or therapy that touches on root issues but have no spiritual power to actually heal, renew or transform, and make whole.

Abused and wounded people, including Christians tend to develop a self-pity oriented inner stance along with a fight or flight (revenge or victim) hidden agenda for living.

Symptoms of a crushed spirit can be very debilitating, making it difficult to live in hope and peace. Satan capitalizes on ignorance and hardness of heart to maintain a strong grip through pity and self-pity.

Jesus had compassion on the wounded and crippled. Because of the abuse he suffered he is able to communicate empathy with those who struggle with a wounded and crushed spirit.

Unfortunately, most in the world, in secular psychology and many Christian counseling ministries patronize the wounded with pity—keeping those crushed in spirit dependent, weak, and wallowing in self-pity.

Jesus shines his light into the inner recesses of the heart and spirit, if allowed by those suffering from hardness of heart and a crushed spirit. This process of breaking the hardness is painful and Jesus will not pity those that come to him, but rather he disciplines in comfort and with encouragement until the hardness and denial is broken. Christ knows the truth and will have compassion on the those who finally experience brokenness of a hardened spirit and become contrite in heart.

Pity was exactly how Satan approached Jesus in the wilderness temptation, trying to get our Lord to feel sorry for himself. The devil tempted him to use his position as the Son of God to command rocks to turn into loaves of bread during the height of Christ's physical hunger.

Even on the cross one of the two thieves railed at Jesus, trying to get Jesus to exercise His power to get all three out of their execution.

Those who suffer from a crushed spirit and a hardened heart must resist the temptation to wallow in self-pity—a devilish inspired condition where God is often internally blamed for a *raw deal in life*.

Many Christians who suffer from a crushed spirit love God and Christ superficially, but in their secret heart, they are angry at God and blame him for life's miseries.

When one comes before Christ asking for help but is in denial of their inner bitter issues and hardened in heart, Christ will have to allow trouble to mount up in life to break denial of a hardened heart. When a broken hardened spirit and contrite heart is experienced, with repentance, Christ will apply true comfort and compassion, minus patronizing pity.

Counterfeit Gifts and False Movements
Angel of Light Spiritual Prozac

Unfortunately, people that are crushed in spirit come to church, fellowship, or a so-called anointed ministry looking to be delivered of their troubled and unstable life, only to receive a spiritual placebo or at best temporary relief from the symptoms.

The symptoms are like warning lights on the dashboard of an automobile signaling the operator to take action and prevent severe damage to the engine.

Sleepless nights, nightmares, mood swings, emotional outbursts, migraines, obsessive lifestyle, compulsions, addictions, sinful habits, weird or evil thoughts, combative relationships, lack of inner peace, hysterical outbursts, phobias, lack of energy, and depression—the list of maladies and chronic emotional and mental challenges are very long.

Most Charismatic, Pentecostal and Evangelical Christians are told that these symptoms are demonic in nature and those who suffer as such are victims that need deliverance from demonic harassment.

In addition to deliverance, the troubled believer needs a fresh "anointing" from a "gifted and anointed" leader who will bestow the "anointing" upon the sufferer. These false Holy Ghost "anointing" experiences often do replace troubled thoughts and disturbing feelings with ecstatic feelings, (often described as sensuous and blissful). However, the ecstatic feelings eventually wear off and soon another encounter or dose from an anointed ministry is required.

This is the work of what is termed "angel of light ministries," stemming from the Apostle Paul's explanation found in his second letter to the Christians at Corinth.

Paul had to teach these misguided Christians about false leaders who mislead Christians, explaining that: *"For such men are false apostles, deceitful workmen, disguising themselves as apostles of Christ. And no wonder, for even Satan disguises himself as an angel of light. So it is not strange if his servants also disguise themselves as servants of righteousness. Their end will correspond to their deeds"* (2 Corinthians 11:13-15).

Today, Christianity has become inundated with false leaders who teach false doctrine and walk in a counterfeit faith empowered by Satan (appearing as an angel of light).

These walk in a counterfeit anointing that manifest false signs and wonders and spiritually convey spiritual but empty manifestations that produce temporary emotional and spiritual highs that affect the nervous system, one's personal spirit, and emotions.

These false ministries dispense manifestations like the many psychiatrists who proscribe Prozac to relieve various mental anguish and other emotional symptoms.

Christians fall for these false manifestations in an attempt to relieve the pressure that is actually allowed by God to get their attention.

The Lord is allowing Satan and inner turmoil to break denial and cause the sincere Christian to take a serious look within and begin to break the layers of hardness that covers a wounded-crushed spirit and a sorrowful heart.

Note: The true gifts of the Holy Spirit are to be exercised by sincere disciples who are trained and dead to carnal motives and glory seeking ambition.

Re-Breaking a Broken Spirit

In Psalm 51 David wrote, *"The sacrifice acceptable to God is a broken spirit; a broken and contrite heart, O God, thou wilt not despise"* (Psalm 51:17).

This passage may seem to be in conflict with the other Scriptures concerning a wounded-crushed spirit. But often, someone suffering from a crushed and wounded spirit also suffers from a hardened spirit, such as a stubborn, willful, or an arrogant spirit. Through years of survival, learning to cope, and advancing somewhat successfully in life, the person's crushed spirit mends wrongly over time.

A good analogy would be like a person lost in the wilderness and suffers a broken leg. Unable to set the broken leg properly and protect the leg with a splint, the bone grows back together wrong. When the person finally makes their way out to civilization with a limp, the medical team will have to re-break the leg and set it properly.

This is often the case as David expressed in the psalm; one must allow their wounded, but hardened spirit to become broken, so that God can work with the believer and expose hidden issues, defilement, roots of bitterness, and festering wounds to the spirit and associated damaged emotions.

Truth in the Inward Being

Another passage from Psalm 51 helps further in understanding how the Lord works in dealing with hidden issues is: *"Behold, thou desirest truth in the inward being; therefore teach me wisdom in my secret heart. Purge me with hyssop, and I shall be clean; wash me, and I shall be whiter than snow"* (Psalm 51:6, 7).

A major key for recovering from a crushed spirit is choosing to see the root issues within the heart and truthfully examining our inner motives and intentions in every aspect of life. Many times we hide from the truth concerning why we feel and do the things we do.

Another potent passage concerning the Lord pressing His people who are crushed in spirit is as follows: *"For the word of God is living and active, sharper than any two-edged sword, piercing to the division of soul and spirit, of joints and marrow, and discerning the thoughts and intentions of the heart. And before him no creature is hidden, but all are open and laid bare to the eyes of him with whom we have to do"* (Hebrews 4:12, 13).

If we cooperate with God in looking at our true motives for feeling and acting the way we do, then the Lord is able to use the written word of God to guide us in exposing carnal selfish motives, and hidden agendas such as jealousy, spitefulness, selfishness, hate, and even murderous thoughts and intentions of the heart.

God sees and knows exactly what our issues are, the problem is we cannot see what he sees, and unfortunately most do not want to know the truth about self from God's perspective.

If we learn to love the truth and ask God to show us exactly what is wrong, He will be faithful and bring to light all that is hidden within—at the right time.

We must learn about this process employed by God; how he breaks our denial and hardness of heart to show us what is hidden. We must choose to cooperate when these painful issues and defilements are brought to our attention.

When we desire truth in the inward being then God is given opportunity to cleanse, purify, heal, and restore us on the inside—and transform our character to be Christ-like in nature.

The Cleansing and Healing Process

Again, this process is called sanctification and transformation. Once we truly believe in Christ, submit to his lordship and learn sound doctrine from Scripture, and fellowship with likeminded Christians—then we will be led by the Holy Spirit into a season of difficulties and challenges that will expose what is hidden within.

There are biblical principles that we must adhere to in order to get through this process with the least amount of trouble and discipline from the Lord. We cannot speed up this process, but we can certainly slow it down by not cooperating, or by maintaining denial, or by staying ignorant.

The first step is learning how to cooperate and then actually doing it. There will be many times that you will find yourself bucking, stuck in a stubborn area of heart, or lack courage in facing certain issues painful wounds. Christ knows all about these areas, He knows our weaknesses, and he is able to empathize, comfort, and encourage—and he knows how to turn the heat up to get our attention and get us moving in the right direction.

When you realize that you have slacked off, rebelled, or just got tired and temporarily given up, or become tempted and overtaken by an old sinful habit—do not wallow in self-pity or condemn yourself, you are under God's grace and mercy.

Part of this work is breaking our denial of just how sinful and needy we really are and to prevent us from being tricked into becoming self-righteous and legalistic, like so many.

If you love Christ and truth, regardless of how many times you get bucked off the horse, get back on.

Submit and Draw Near to God

The first step is to submit yourself to the absolute Lordship of Christ and give him permission to do whatever it takes to bring you the fullness of life in Him— and be willing to experience His plan for your life come to pass.

In submitting, you must learn to seek him and draw near to him—then and only then he will draw near to you.

Many things in this life distract us from following and obeying Christ. Most are legitimate things that we must do and partake in. Some are things that give us enjoyment, rest and refreshment, having entertaining value.

However, in this age of prosperity and ease, we tend to idolize blessings to the point that they become a curse and actually distract us. Many go to church only to be entertained, learning to worship God in rote, giving God lip service.

In the book of James it states, *"You do not have, because you do not ask. You ask and do not receive, because you ask wrongly, to spend it on your passions. Unfaithful creatures! Do you not know that friendship with the world is enmity with God? Therefore whoever wishes to be a friend of the world makes himself an enemy of God"* (James 4:2-4).

Do not be unfaithful to God, like so many by being in love with this world and its deceitful pleasures.

A special note: If it is possible find a like-minded ministry or fellowship where leadership provides pastoral counsel and Christian workers who have been trained by the Lord to hear from the Holy Spirt in revealing hidden issues of heart.

The Apostle Paul wrote concerning the gift of prophesy being an important work of a recovery ministry within fellowship, *"But if all prophesy, and an unbeliever or outsider enters, he is convicted by all, he is called to account by all, the secrets of his heart are disclosed, and so, falling on his face, he will worship God and declare that God is really among you.* (1 Corinthians 14:24-25).

Resisting the Devil

Satan will oppose you just about every step of the way. As long as a Christian is playing church and following false doctrine that helps maintain denial and hardness—Satan usually leaves that deceived Christian alone.

Once one wakes up and draws near to God in all seriousness, the devil will come out of the woodwork, when you least expect it. It is the serious saint that the devil fears and be assured Satan will be allowed to harass and attack. However, trust God for the Lord will always have the final say.

The devil is a tool in God's hand for the work of sanctification and transformation, like a junkyard dog on a chain that is measured to the very inch.

You will get bitten by the devil if you stray into areas that hinder your growth. When we procrastinate and disobey, we can expect the devil's heat.

Fiery trials expose hidden issues, impurity, and weak character—and also builds faith in Christ as we learn to trust in Him and not ourselves.

As we face these trials and attacks in faith and trust in God, we learn to deal with our "gunk" that comes to the surface—unbelief, bad attitude, roots of bitterness, and lack of courage etc. As we gain strength and purity, we also see character changes and increased self-discipline, wisdom, and more attributes of a holy, content, peaceful, and *fruit of the Spirit* filled life.

So, learn how to identify the devil's schemes and be prepared to resist the devil, standing firm in your faith. You will not be put through more than your faith can handle, although it will seem too hard and overwhelming at times. You will suffer and in the suffering resist self-pity and false doctrine that says Christians are exempt from suffering.

"Resist him, firm in your faith, knowing that the same experience of <u>suffering is required of your brotherhood throughout the world</u>. And after you have <u>suffered a little while</u>, the God of all grace, who has called you to his eternal glory in Christ, will himself <u>restore, establish, and strengthen you</u>. To him be the dominion forever and ever. Amen" (1 Peter 5:9, 10 underline added).

Of course, always look to Jesus and how he suffered for us. (See Hebrews 12:1-17.)

Purifying the Heart

When we first respond to Christ and the Holy Spirit's call to salvation, most of us were filled with repentance and joy. A new peace settled in our hearts and all seemed well as we learned more about Christ, our Heavenly Father, and the Holy Spirit, the Scriptures, fellowship and sound doctrine that promotes maturity.

As stated earlier, many are told that any overwhelming temptation, problems, emotional issues, bad thoughts, disturbing feelings, or backsliding into sin is of the devil or lack of faith.

To the contrary, as mentioned previously, these are indicators of impurity within the heart. Bad feelings, wrong thoughts, poor attitudes, and sinful behavior—all stem from an impure heart that carries unbelief or misbeliefs about God, self, and others.

To best describe how impurities of the heart lay hidden after one becomes a believer, I will use one of my own experiences where trials and pressing circumstances exposed a deep wound and impurity hidden within my heart for years:

There are many accounts to choose from, but the one that is most memorable is when the Lord showed me a misbelief that I had harbored in my heart about God. This occurred in 1987, fourteen years after I became a Christian.

I started counseling with a pastor who worked in a faith ministry. It was a 100-mile round trip and those he counseled gave what they could afford in the form of an honorarium.

One day I came to my session frustrated with God. In fact, I pounded on the pastor's desk and asked, "Where is God? It's like five steps forward, ten back."

Carl was the pastor's name, a big burly man, and full of the love of God. He motioned that he understood, held his hand up to stop my rant, and then he started thumbing through his notes. About a minute later, with a puzzled look on his face, he said, "Chuck, I'm depending on the Holy Spirit here, I don't see this in my notes." And then he asked, "Did your father ever tell you he wanted to kill you?"

When he said this, a memory flashed into my thoughts. I had never shared that with him or any other. This was something hidden deep in my heart for years. I said, "Yes, many times he would chase me and my brother into a corner, from five years old and up, shake his fist and threaten to kill us, right then and there!"

Carl looked at me intently and said, "Our relationship with our Heavenly Father is initially founded in our relationship with our earthly father. You have taken that fear and rejection from these death threats in early childhood and transferred them to your relationship with your Heavenly Father. In your secret heart you believe that God wants to kill you, too!"

It was as if a light turned on. It made sense. I know now it was the Holy Spirit bearing witness to what the Lord was having Carl prophesy. The Holy Spirit drew out of my heart a forgotten wound and brought it to my conscious awareness. (Again, see the Apostle Paul's teaching on the true gift of prophecy in 1 Corinthians 14:20-25 where secrets of the heart are to be exposed).

He followed up by saying, "That is not true of God. You have unbelief in your heart, which is sin." He continued, "You need to repent."

I could feel pressure in my heart as Carl led me in a simple prayer of repentance. When I finished praying, I wept and wept. It was like a ton of bricks had been lifted off my heart and spirit.

Carl stood by me as I continued to weep. I felt like jelly inside and became physically weak. Carl gave me a bear hug to give comfort, which also helped to physically stabilize me (literally, my legs felt that weak). We finished that session and I continued to weep on and off during the drive home.

This account I refer as one of the first of many "open heart surgeries" that the Holy Spirit performed upon me in my own recovery in Christ.

Some hidden impurities may carry extreme pain, anger, and sorrow. The following passage from James is the biblical principle at work with the account I just described.

"Submit yourselves therefore to God. Resist the devil and he will flee from you. Draw near to God and he will draw near to you. Cleanse your hands, you sinners, and purify your hearts, you men of double mind. Be wretched and mourn and weep. Let your laughter be turned to mourning and your joy to dejection. Humble yourselves before the Lord and he will exalt you" (James 4:7-10).

We must humble ourselves and pay attention to the symptoms and pursue the Lord for answers. He is faithful to reveal the unresolved issues buried within our heart and spirit.

Overcoming a Crushed Spirit and Dividedness

In the passage from James just quoted, the author mentions double-mindedness (a two souled condition).

Overcoming a twice-a-soul and a crushed spirit condition requires understanding of dividedness and fragmentation. The following are some terms and definitions to become familiar with:

Splitting Process: Trauma from abuse often causes a splitting and shattering process in one's personal spirit that often mixes with damaged emotions holding painful memories from the trauma. This splitting process is the cycle of nature or wheel of birth James speaks about that creates a split or alternate personality. This process of splitting is an automatic defense/survival mechanism that walls off the trauma (memory and pain) until resolution and healing can happen later when one is older and more mature—when one can process what happened in the truth of Christ.

Split Personalities: If trauma from physical, sexual, or emotional abuse continues, and depending on the intensity, to survive as a child or even an adult, a human being can create a complex system of divided parts in the form of whole, partial, and fragmented personalities. These personalities that can emerge at different times to help the victim manage life (sometimes normally), survive, fight, rebel, undermine, or flee life's challenges.

Set on Fire by Hell: The demonic can infest and cohabitate in the split parts of the soul and spirit, they can stay hidden, or return later in life, even after one becomes born-again. The demonic or demons then harasses and attacks, and often burrows in and cohabitates in the split parts of the personal spirit.

Counterbalancing Division: Depending on the degree of abuse and length of time, a birthing and developing of counterbalancing personalities occurs along the lines of negative emotions and behavior (revengeful, bitterness, etc.), and then opposite or counterbalancing personalities are developed with positive behavior (caring, helpful, etc.). These opposing sets of personalities produce instability and vacillating between good and bad thoughts and good and bad feelings. Christians who struggle in this condition have split personalities that house narcissism, bitter jealousy, selfish ambition and other negative attitudes along with raw and damaged emotions that support wrong motives in life. These personalities can operate subtly in the background and create disorder, act out inappropriate behaviors, and create a devilish atmosphere in marriage and in family and fellowship (James 3:13-18). Several major symptoms are mood swings, uncontrolled outbursts of anger and manipulative behavior.

A Double Heart: Some with a *twice-a-soul* condition can be split within their core or in the heart This leaves a large portion of their inner self-life full anger, fear, unbelief, extreme self-centeredness, and evil thinking. Yet, they may have an outer persona that attempts to seek God and a desire to live righteously. Some become so enraged at life and at God that they choose to not believe in God and abandon their faith, blaming God or believing there is no God. A large portion of their heart embedded in bitterness and unbelief, which is often deeply hidden. And sometimes later in life they want to believe in God again—but without dealing with their true feelings and beliefs hidden within their double heart they run into a brick wall. This type of severe splitting is the most difficult condition to overcome. Secular psychology identifies this as schizophrenia. (Hebrews 3:12-14; 12:15-17).

Emerging Roots of Bitterness: Submerged personalities are often soaked in unresolved anger, rage, bitter jealousy, resentment, fear, self-pity, and revenge can develop into roots of bitterness that spring up, cause trouble, and physically, emotionally as well as spiritually defile others.

Alternating Personalities and Equilibrium: A juggling system is developed by most in a *twice-a-soul* condition. Automatic equilibrium is maintained by a subtle cueing and juggling of alternate personalities. Different personalities emerge and take control depending on life's challenges. Denial of *twice-a-soul* condition is often broken during a crisis when the juggling system breaks down and equilibrium is lost.

Crisis of Life Causing Mental and Emotional Breakdown: Apostle Peter went through a crisis of life that broke his denial of a *twice-a-soul* condition. When he saw the truth and remembered Christ's warnings, that he would deny Christ three times, Peter wept bitterly. (Luke 22:31-34; 52-62). Fortunately, Jesus had prayed that Peter's faith would not fail completely in this crisis. Many divided people meet a crisis and lose faith and lose their grip on reality because they do not understand what is happening. Far too many believe the lies of the devil and the world's answers to their condition. They become stuck in a breakdown of equilibrium, resulting in all kinds of neurotic or emotional imbalances. The science of psychology tries to help by categorizing these results but it fails to take into account the power of almighty God, the human spirit, sin, the demonic, and the inner duality of the sin nature, faith, and the desire to live righteously.

Some Have Crossed Over to the Dark Side
Avoid Such People

Many who have been abused give up the good fight, reject their conscience as well as their faith. In the end many stuck in this downward spiraling process of moving towards evil, they cross over completely into darkness.

The evil perpetrated against them, along with the devil's beckoning call misleads many to fight evil with evil. For those who cross over, most believe that God abandoned them to evil, and thus rebel against God and righteousness.

The criminally evil person is obvious for most to see, as many go on crime sprees in a rage against society, filled with hatred and hatred of self.

However, the most dangerous evil are those who chose to stay in an internal self-righteous stance, becoming totally narcissistic. This type of evil person often becomes very religious, driven entirely by selfish motives.

The Apostle Paul warned about this by writing, *"For such persons do not serve our Lord Christ, but their own appetites, and by fair and flattering words they deceive the hearts of the simple-minded* [1]. *For while your obedience is known to all, so that I rejoice over you, I would have you wise as to what is good and guileless as to what is evil; then the God of peace will soon crush Satan under your feet. The grace of our Lord Jesus Christ be with you"* (Romans 16:18-20).

There are many references in Scripture concerning those who give up their faith, crossed over to darkness, and yet appear to be good. The above passage Paul exhorts: *"Avoid them"* (Romans 16:17).

Further, Paul wrote to Timothy identifying such people, again warning *"Avoid such people"* (2 Timothy 3:5). The Apostle Peter referred to these so-called Christians as *"accursed children"* (See 2 Peter 2:1-22). In Jude, this New Testament author called this type of person, *"waterless clouds, fruitless trees, grumblers, malcontents, and loud-mouthed boasters, flatterers, worldly people devoid of the Spirit"* (see Jude 12-19).

Then we must remember and understand that Judas Iscariot was a prime example, in which Jesus referred to as *"the son of perdition."* Even though Christ knew that Judas was a devil from the beginning and warned the disciples of the threat in general terms—the disciples did not realize what Christ meant until the actual betrayal took place.

Wounded Christians tend to become closely involved with this type of person and find themselves hampered by the darkness that hides behind flattery and false goodness.

---

[1] Simple Minded: In the context of this passage and proper translation simple minded means naïve, inexperienced, gullible, and immature.

Christ warned that at the end of this age Satan would plant evil weeds among the wheat. Thus, we must learn to detect through proper discernment human devils implanted by Satan himself—in the midst of fellowships and congregations everywhere. (See the parable of the weeds in Matthew 13:24-43.)

Part of overcoming a crushed spirit is choosing to be around true Christians and avoiding those who have crossed over to the dark side. Discernment is a major key in recovery and growth, and is developed through sound doctrine presented by leaders who have become true disciples of Christ, led by the Holy Spirit.

When those crushed in spirit become trained in their understanding about evil and realize how evil people in their past helped crush their spirit—sensitivity and awareness becomes more keen in detecting those who are currently in their lives who have evil intent and who subtly practice wickedness.

Old habits and bad relationships must be broken off. In some cases, these people may be close relatives; nevertheless, proper boundaries must be put in place to help protect recovery and maintain spiritual and emotional cleanliness, healthy relationships and maturity in Christ—therefore learn to *avoid such people.*

Jesus taught that we must be willing to give up any unhealthy relationship ties if we are to successfully follow him. In fact, Christ said we must hate these unhealthy relationships because most become idolatrous, where family and sometimes loved one who have an agenda to control others often cause trouble and do not have our best interest in mind, but rather continue to use and abuse their relationships. Review Christ's teaching on this in Luke 14:25-34.

Wholeness and Christ-like Character

The results of going through this sanctification and recovery process are newness of life, new feelings, and the fruit of the Holy Spirit with love, joy, and peace pervading the inner person. A deep sense of oneness with God the Father will be felt as well. (See Galatians 5:22-24; Romans 6:5-8; John 10:10).

To help facilitate and maintain stability of the new life and newly changed character, those in recovery will need to follow some simple guidelines. This will ensure solid footing when the wounded gain some stability and begin to grow in grace with God.

Wounded believers need to be exposed to a loving Christian environment, to share with, learn from, and where burden bearing becomes a vital part of the body of Christ's nurturing, mentoring, accountability processes.

In many cases a true body of believers takes on the role as emotional and spiritual first aid workers and instruments of spiritual and emotional healing in God's hands. Many who had abusive parents receive godly father and mother care where fellowship fulfils a Holy Spirit led re-parenting ministry.

The Apostle Paul wrote: *"I do not write this to make you ashamed, but to admonish you as my beloved children. For though you have countless guides in Christ, you do not have many fathers. For I became your father in Christ Jesus through the gospel. I urge you, then, be imitators of me"* (1 Corinthians 4:14-16).

We all need to continue in the word of God, seeking God's will and ever growing in His grace and peace, and more so for those in recovery.

Many Christians get some healing from the Lord and then because of the newly found stability, abandon the desire to continue to grow in a deeper relationship with Christ. Jesus warned that going all the way with Him and becoming a true disciple is difficult but a grave responsibility.

Like the 10 lepers Christ healed, only one came back and fell at the Master's feet and worshipped Him as Healer and Lord (See Luke 17:11-19.) Also—*"For this very reason make every effort to supplement your faith with virtue, and virtue with knowledge, and knowledge with self-control, and self-control with steadfastness, and steadfastness with godliness, and godliness with brotherly affection and brotherly affection with love. For if these things are yours and abound, they keep you from being ineffective or unfruitful in the knowledge of our Lord Jesus Christ"* (2 Pet. 1:5-8).

Remember, Jesus said: *"Ask, and it will be given you; seek, and you will find; knock, and it will be opened to you. For everyone who asks receives, and he who seeks finds, and to him who knocks it will be opened. Or what man of you, if his son asks him for bread, will give him a stone? Or if he asks for a fish, will give him a serpent? If you then, who are evil, know how to give good gifts to your children, how much more will your Father who is in heaven give good things to those who ask him"* (Matthew 7:7-11).

We must learn to abide in Christ, setting our minds in heavenly places, learning to be led by the Holy Spirit.

"Abide in me, and I in you. As the branch cannot bear fruit by itself, unless it abides in the vine, neither can you, unless you abide in me... If you abide in me, and my words abide in you, ask whatever you will, and it shall be done for you" (John 15:4-7).

Many Christians wonder how one can abide in Christ and still interact with people, engage in work, and function in society without appearing or acting weird.

The Apostle Paul wrote, *"To set the mind on the flesh is death, but to set the mind on the Spirit is life and peace. For the mind that is set on the flesh is hostile to God; it does not submit to God's law, indeed it cannot; and those who are in the flesh cannot please God. But you are not in the flesh, you are in the Spirit, if in fact the Spirit of God dwells in you. Anyone who does not have the Spirit of Christ does not belong to him"* (Romans 8:6-9).

Setting our mind on the Spirit of God can seem impossible and rightly so if we do not understand and embrace the work of the cross. In another passage Paul writes, *"If then you have been raised with Christ, seek the things that are above, where Christ is, seated at the right hand of God. Set your minds on things that are above, not on things that are on earth. For you have died, and your life is hid with Christ in God. When Christ who is our life appears, then you also will appear with him in glory. Put to death therefore what is earthly in you: fornication, impurity, passion, evil desire, and covetousness, which is idolatry."* (Colossians 3:1-5).

Having the works of the flesh and the carnal nature brought to death is a process that transforms our mind and heart (even as wounded Christians), nullifying the power of the old nature and enabling the ability to sense the Spirit's presence at all times.

If you suffer from a crushed spirit or just a wounded spirit, then crucifying the works of the flesh will be impossible. One's wounded spirit will continue to cling to the things of this world, relationships, and false religion unable and unwilling to trust God. However, once a crushed spirit begins to be healed, (in the healing process the works of the flesh will begin to die), and the fullness of life in Christ will become attainable.

The things of this world, desires, and carnal interests can now be controlled and no longer occupy and absorb our attention. We learn to pay attention to things on earth but not have our hearts and minds become preoccupied with earthly and fleshly desires.

An example of abiding in the Spirit and sensing His presence, while engaging in life's demands is as follows:

As we learn to engage in conversation with two or three people, we can maintain awareness with all who are present in the group. If one is talking, we can listen and also hear another speak or interact. We can even learn to pick up on the body language of each within a group discussion with two, three, and even four people. The key to acquiring this ability is learning to listen rather than constantly think about what to say next.

When we seek Christ, understand His words, learn to put off the old nature, and no longer grieve the Holy Spirit, we can learn to sense God's presence. We can learn to abide in His continual presence and listen for His voice while engaging in life's demands.

If we have unresolved emotional issues, defilements within our spirit and lack rest and peace in God, the sensing of His presence becomes overshadowed by these internal issues aggravated by earthly external pressures and events.

Often while working out our salvation and maturing in Christ, one can revert to rebellion and grieve the Holy Spirit. If this happens, the Lord knows how to scold and bring us back to him, if we humble ourselves and repent.

One must learn to repent and deal with the carnal issues that drive us to set our mind on earthly things or on our fleshly desires. When we maintain a continual attitude of repentance without condemning ourselves, then we are able to restore our relationship with the Holy Spirit and go on learning to consistently abide in His presence.

Yes: *"The LORD is near to the brokenhearted, and saves the crushed in spirit"* (Psalm 34:18).

Unfortunately, until we humbly confess our hardness of heart and break denial, those who suffer from a crushed spirit will always push God away. Our hardened hearts refuse His truth and love that, if allowed penetrates to the hidden wounds we don't want to face.

We cover our eyes and pretend all is well as we learn to walk with a veil—a mask that hides the pain from others and from ourselves.

Most who suffer from a crushed spirit feel hopeless; however, with God all things are possible. He is an expert at restoring wholeness to the broken hearted and the crushed in spirit.

A Biblical Healing and Recovery Program

It is highly recommended that those reading this introduction to recovering from a crushed spirit become active in a Biblical healing and recovery program.

If one is not available in your fellowship, present this information to your pastor or church leaders. Training and resources are available to start a solid healing and recovery program. Ministry contact information is found on the last pages of this resource.

It is important that the recovery program is comprised of trained facilitators, counselors, and mentors. In addition, support group facilitation must embrace Biblical principles that address healing and recovery for a two-souled condition where confidentiality, security, and protection from the insincere are high priorities.

A successful Biblical recovery program should be sponsored and supported by a solid fellowship with a core of mature disciples ministering and facilitating the program. The true gifts of the Holy Spirit should also be operation in all wisdom and order.

The following resource will help individuals and groups work through God's recovery processes:

Overcoming Through Christ
God's Recovery Program – Participant's Guidebook
With 40 day Devotional and Personal Journal
ISBN 978-1-943412-22-8

Disclaimer

The Healing and Transforming Power of Christ

We believe Christ can heal wounds to the spirit and the emotional and mental symptoms associated with a crushed spirit. This introduction and the recommended guidebook covers Biblical principles that—when understood and properly applied—will facilitate healing of a wounded spirit, resolved and heal damaged emotions, heal mental anguish, and change to one's inner character. These principles are a direct aid for struggling Christians who want to work out transformation of the old nature and have a new Christ-like nature take its place and walk in the fullness of life in Christ as promised in Scripture.

Wilderness Voice Publishing and the author, Charles Pretlow, <u>do not claim</u> to be a mental health organization or a mental health professional. This material contains Biblical principles and teachings that God has given to help facilitate healing for those who suffer from a wounded or crushed spirit, a broken heart, damaged emotions, and dividedness of soul and spirit.

Implementation of these principles is not a guarantee for healing. Each person is accountable for his or her own relationship with God based on genuine trust and faith in the transforming grace, power, and work of God through His Son, Jesus Christ.

We believe that with the Person of Christ, along with proper understanding of God's word, a struggling believer can be transformed from a wounded, carnally-natured Christian into a Christ-like, new-natured Christian. The carnal nature with its associated wounds and defilements to the personal spirit often carry psychological and emotional symptoms.

Terms used in explaining these principles may have been used or are used in secular counseling, therapy, or training. The use of such terms in explaining these Biblical principles do not indicate or infer that this teaching is a mental health program sanctioned or licensed by any state or national mental health licensing board.

If you are uncomfortable with this Biblical approach in healing spiritual, psychological, emotional wounds, and behavioral issues and you believe you need to be evaluated by a mental health professional, we recommend that you contact your family physician or a mental health referral agency as soon as possible.

About the Author

Pastor Charles Pretlow has nearly three decades of experience in ministry, pastoral counseling, and leadership training. He completed his basic Bible classes at Seattle Pacific College and finished his undergraduate work at Central Washington University in Business Administration and Computer Science.

His military training in leadership and as a military instructor, along with years of coaching athletics adds to a well-rounded approach in leadership instruction, mentoring and training.

It was in 1973, while in the Marines that he came to know Christ and then in 1974 started his ministerial work. Charles has seen much confusion within the body of Christ due to false doctrines that leave many believers confused and bewildered. This terrible condition in Christianity also leads wounded Christians into hopelessness where most give up on Christ. In 1988 Charles answered the call to address these problems and started a counseling and mentoring ministry which led to the foundation of a non-denominational fellowship in 1990.

All these years of ministry has steered Charles to rely on his extensive knowledge and understanding of Scripture, the gifts of the Holy Spirit, and Christ's teachings. The challenges of ministry in difficult times caused him to personally rely the Holy Spirit, bringing him to experience the fullness of Christ. This abiding relationship in Christ emanates a companionate and firm delivery of the Gospel, inspiring those involved in this work to abide in Christ as well.

His preaching, teaching and discerning insights encourages those who have a heart for Christ—yet he is uncompromising concerning the false, the game player, and the wolf.

The main key to Pastor Pretlow's success is embracing Christ's teachings and leadership principles often overlooked or avoided. Years of preaching, teaching, and counseling with gifts of the Holy

Spirit required the need to understand and apply all that Christ taught. He has concluded that the harder words of Christ, when embraced brings death to the carnal self-life, leading to the fullness of life in Christ, and that too many Christians are led to take shortcuts resulting in a weak and often false walk with Christ.

His first published book was in 2004, when he began to write extensively on the sorrowful condition of the body of Christ, the false teachings misleading so many, and the desperate need for true recovery from a crushed spirit and damaged emotions—that can only be worked out in Christ. Having authored over ten titles, he continues to write in a style that is straight forward and to the root issues besetting God's people today.

Currently Charles is part of the Message of the Cross International leadership team and one of the pastors ministering at MC Chapel Fellowship in Canon City, Colorado. He continues to write and speak, helping the sincere Christian prepare for the coming dark times leading up to Christ's appearance.

Recovery Ministry Information

For more information on MCI Recovery Ministries contact us using the following web site: www.mcirecovery.com

To physically participate in MCI Recovery Ministries in Colorado visit us at the following:

Fellowship:	MC Chapel Fellowship
	PO Box 857
	Canon City, CO 81215
Physical location:	MC Chapel Fellowship
	The Abbey/St. Josephs' Building Suite 102
	2951 E. Hwy 50
	Canon City, CO 81212
Email: contact@mccfcanoncity.com - www.mccfcanoncity.com
Telephone:	(888) 575-9626